Snack, Snooze, Skedaddle

SKEDADDLE

HOW ANIMALS GET READY FOR WINTER

LAURA PURDIE SALAS

illustrated by **CLAUDINE GÉVRY**

Ⓜ Millbrook Press / Minneapolis

Soak up the sun, breathe in the breeze,
munch crunchy apples that fall from the trees.
Enjoy every morsel you feast on today:
the banquet of autumn will soon fade away.

So plump up or burrow or journey *before*
frosty winds rattle and batter your door.
Snowstorms and dark nights are next to arrive.
Here comes winter!

PREPARE. SURVIVE!

Dive into snapdragons. Double your size!

Dine on delectable tropical flies.

This ruby-throated hummingbird
puts on weight to power his
long, nonstop flight south.

Float like a kite on a sweet, nectar breeze.

Cluster on branches of tall family trees.

This monarch butterfly flies south in fall
to mate and lay eggs in spring.

Sift krill through your grill
to sustain your great weight.

Sail south to warm waters, and seek out a mate.

This blue whale spends summer in cold northern waters but travels south to tropical waters to breed in the winter.

Vacuum dead leaves like
a super-slow sweeper.

Forget going south. Just wiggle down deeper!

As soil freezes, this earthworm burrows down below the layer of frozen ground.

Hide away seeds as your winter stash grows.

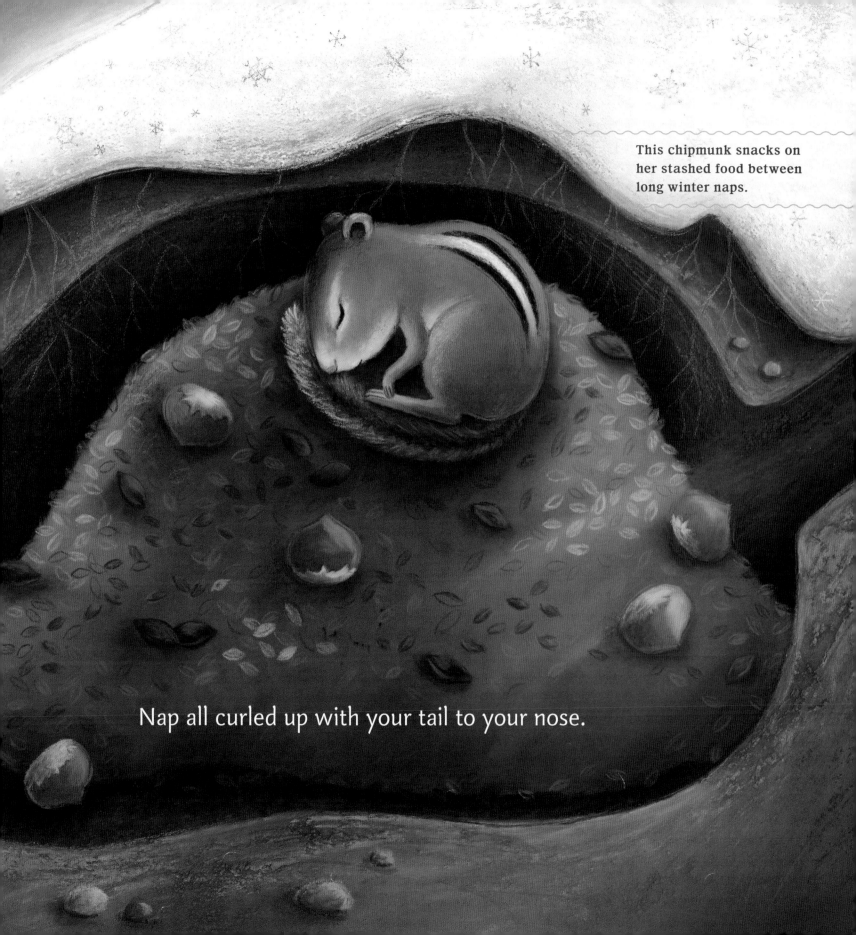

This chipmunk snacks on her stashed food between long winter naps.

Nap all curled up with your tail to your nose.

Gobble up acorns and beechnuts by streams.

This black bear's fall feast
sustains his body all winter.

Snooze through the winter in hazelnut dreams.

Tuck under leaves. Don't rustle. Don't hop.

All life signs have stopped—
you're a frog icy pop!

This frozen Northern wood frog stops breathing for months, then thaws and hops away!

Slither and bask. Stay solo.
Stay single.

This garter snake snuggles with thousands of friends to share body heat.

Swarm with some friends. It's warmer to mingle.

Stock up your pantries with dried seeds and scraps.

Hope that your tunnel doesn't collapse!

This mouse scurries through snowy tunnels to reach her food caches—and she hopes a fox doesn't drop in!

Grow a new coat that's cozy and warm.

Stay toasty no matter
how brutal the storm!

This moose wears fur all year, but he grows special hollow
hairs in winter that trap warm air against his body.

Forage for berries and
crabapple sweets.

The red fox dives headlong into the snow to catch voles, mice, and other small mammals to stay well-fed all winter.

Dive into tunnels for tasty vole treats.

Jump into jumbled-up
piles of gold.

Spin, skate, and slide through the frosty, white cold.

We humans living where winters are cold bundle up and have fun!

THREE SURVIVAL STRATEGIES

Animals have many amazing skills and traits that help them survive winter. Survival strategies usually fall into three categories: migrate, hibernate, or tolerate.

MIGRATE

When animals migrate, they travel to a different location at a certain time of year. Often, animals' food supply dies off or goes underground for the winter. So some animals travel to a warmer place to find food. Other animals cannot survive the frigid temperatures of winter and migrate to warmer places. Still others migrate because they will mate and have young in spring, and their newborns have a better chance of survival in a warmer place where food is more abundant.

In winter, most migrating animals journey across land or sea in the direction of the equator. This imaginary line around the middle of the earth receives direct sunlight all year long. But some animals migrate vertically, or up and down. Earthworms move deeper into the soil as the ground freezes, and bighorn sheep and mountain goats move down from mountains peaks. The sheep and mountain goats spend the winter down lower where plants are still growing.

HIBERNATE

When animals hibernate, they depress their metabolism. That means their heartbeat slows, their breathing slows, and their body temperature lowers. This physical state of lowered metabolism is called torpor. An animal is said to hibernate if it spends at least several days in a row in a state of torpor.

Usually, animals hibernate because food is less available and low air temperatures demand more energy from their bodies. An animal in torpor does not need much food. And its body slows down so much it uses very little energy.

An animal in torpor does not simply let its body temperature fall with outside temperatures. Torpor is the physical (though invisible) act of slowing down all body functions. Torpor is not the same thing as being asleep, though we often say hibernating animals "sleep" or "nap" through the winter. It is actually a very distinct physical state.

Different hibernators behave in different ways. Some store body fat; others don't. Some rouse to eat and drink over the hibernation period; others don't. Some hibernate for a month; others hibernate for six months. Even the way the same species behaves in different parts of the country varies a lot. Torpor is the common bond. All hibernating animals spend much of their time in torpor.

Scientists don't fully understand the process of going into torpor and rousing from torpor. Their questions include: How do animals know when it's time to go into torpor? What signals them that it's time to rouse?

TOLERATE

Animals that tolerate winter don't migrate or hibernate. Instead, they adapt to the season. They might change the way they look or grow a warmer coat. They might change their diet, based on what food is available. They might change their feeding or hunting tactics because of the snow on the ground. They might become communal in order to share body heat, even though they are solitary the rest of the year. If they're human animals, they might put on mittens, jackets, and hats before they go outside! And they might celebrate winter with sports and games they can only play when there is snow or ice.

VARIATIONS

Within a single species, males and females usually use the same survival skills. Both male and female monarch butterflies migrate to warmer spots for winter, for example. But different populations of monarchs migrate to different locations. Monarchs that live in the eastern United States mostly migrate to Mexico. Monarchs living in the western United States mostly migrate to a particular area in California. Different populations of humans behave differently too. People living in Maine might tolerate winter by wearing a warm, heavy coat, while people in Louisiana might need only a light jacket to tolerate winter.

Do you use any winter survival skills? Which ones?

AMARING SURVIVORS! 〜〜〜〜〜〜〜〜〜〜〜〜〜〜

Let's get to know the animals you met earlier in the book and see the different ways they migrate, hibernate, and tolerate. Although each note describes one specific example of the animal and calls it "he" or "she," the survival strategy described is used by both males and females of that species.

MIGRATORS

RUBY-THROATED HUMMINGBIRD

The ruby-throated hummingbird lives on flower nectar and insects. During most of the year, he weighs about 0.1 ounces (3 grams), the same as a US penny. But in fall, the tiny bird almost doubles his weight. By the time he begins his nonstop flight to Mexico or Central America, he might weigh as much as a US quarter! He needs the extra body weight for energy, since he might fly 1,200 miles (1,900 kilometers) without stopping once.

MONARCH BUTTERFLY

This monarch butterfly drifts around, sipping on nectar. But as winter nears, she stops drifting and flies in a straight line about 3,000 miles (4,800 kilometers) south to central Mexico. There she finds the same habitat where her ancestors spent the winter in past years. Tens of millions of monarchs migrate to gather in the forests on several mountains. She clusters with others for warmth and rests for the winter. In spring, she will fly to the southern United States, mate, lay eggs, and die. Her offspring will migrate north, but it will take several generations to complete the trip.

BLUE WHALE

The blue whale is the largest animal ever to have lived—even bigger than the biggest dinosaur! Though this whale weighs 150–200 tons (136–181 metric tons), he eats tiny, shrimplike krill. Through his bristly baleen plates, he eats up to 4 tons (4 metric tons) of krill daily. He lives in the chilly waters of the North Pacific Ocean, but he and many others swim south for the winter where the females will give birth. In winter, he will continue to gorge on krill in the warm waters near Mexico or Central America.

EARTHWORM

Not all migration moves from north to south. Some earthworms migrate vertically! This one starts out in shallow soil. As the topsoil begins to freeze, the worm wriggles its way deeper underground, where the soil doesn't freeze. This is called vertical migration. Scientists believe that once earthworms are deeper in the soil, they remain inactive for the winter.

HIBERNATORS

CHIPMUNK

This chipmunk eats more food to gain extra body fat for winter, and she also gathers seeds and other foods and stores them underground. In winter, she lives in her underground den. She goes into torpor for several days at a time, but then she rouses to nibble on stored food. In deep torpor, her heart rate slows from 350 beats per minute to around 4 beats per minute! She might not leave her den for the entire winter. Or on warm days, she might come out of her den to stretch in the winter sun.

BEAR

In summer and early fall, this black bear might gain as much as 20–30 pounds (9–14 kilograms) per WEEK by feasting on nuts. Then he waddles into his winter den. His heartbeat slows and he spends most of winter in a state of torpor. Although he might rouse several times, he does not eat or drink. Instead, his body uses up the extra fat he gained in autumn. Come spring, when the world around turns green and food is available again, this bear will emerge from his den skinny—and hungry!

NORTHERN WOOD FROG

The Northern wood frog takes hibernation to an extreme level by freezing into a solid block! Before she freezes, large amounts of natural sugars circulate through her body. These sugars act like antifreeze and keep the water inside her body's cells from freezing. But the water in the spaces *between* the cells does freeze. With more than two-thirds of the water in her body turning to ice, she looks like an ice cube. She doesn't breathe or move, and her heart doesn't even beat! Winter passes, and the wood frog just lies there—easy freezy. But when the temperature warms up in spring, she will thaw and hop away, unharmed.

GARTER SNAKE

Most of the year, this garter snake is solitary. But in winter, if a small den deep below the frost line isn't available, some cold-climate garter snakes get a little help from their friends. In fall, this snake travels to his winter hibernation spot, called a hibernaculum. Once he arrives, he slides into the large underground den with lots of other snakes. Shared body heat helps them all survive bitter winter temperatures. At one spot in Manitoba, Canada, tens of thousands of snakes gather in a den that might be about the size of a living room.

TOLERATORS

MOUSE

This busy mouse spends all autumn stocking up for winter. She gathers corn, wheat, cherry pits, acorns, and other tasty bits and tucks them away in different spots for times when food is scarce. Once winter arrives, she spends most of her time in the subnivium. That's the zone that can form between the ground and the snow that has fallen on it. The lowest layer of snow sometimes melts, leaving spaces with a snowy roof. The mouse finds air pockets and creates tunnels below the snow's surface, and the snowy blanket all around keeps her nice and warm. She scampers from one food cache to another, but she has to be careful. Some predators, like the red fox, have such fine hearing that they can hear small animals below the snow. A fox will dive headfirst into the snow, collapsing the mouse's tunnel to catch a tasty treat.

MOOSE

Mammals constantly grow new hair. Some animals change their hair color in winter to blend in with their surroundings. Not moose! He changes his hair in another way. In summer, his guard hairs, or outer hairs, are solid. But in winter, they grow in as hollow hairs, like straws. His hairs slurp up heat from the sun and deliver it to his woolly undercoat. The warm undercoat next to his skin keeps him toasty warm. He might even start to pant if the temperature gets up to 25°F (4°C) in the winter!

RED FOX

This red fox is an omnivore, so she eats whatever she can find. In summer and fall, she uses her strong eyesight, great sense of smell, and keen hearing to find food. She stalks and chases small mammals and dines on fruits, plants, nuts, and insects too. She sometimes stores a little food for winter. Once snow covers the ground, though, acute hearing is her greatest weapon. She can hear a vole or mouse that is 100 yards (91 m) away scratching for food in tunnels below the snow! She trots to the spot, crouches, leaps, and then plunges deep into the snow to catch her dinner.

HUMAN

We humans who live where winters are cold have lots of survival options. We don't hibernate, but we might stay under cozy blankets a long time. We don't migrate, but we might stay inside heated buildings or take a trip somewhere hot. And we can tolerate winter by wearing warmer clothes (and maybe even drinking hot cocoa). With the right equipment and clothing, we can even celebrate winter while we ice-skate, play hockey, ski, snowshoe, and build snow forts!

GLOSSARY

antifreeze: a substance in a liquid that lowers the temperature that the liquid freezes at. It allows liquids to stay liquid in cold temperatures.

baleen plates: curtainlike, bristly combs that hang from a whale's top jaw and are used to trap krill inside its mouth

bask: to get or stay warm using a heat source, such as sunlight

delectable: delicious

equator: an imaginary line around the middle of the earth, equally distant from the North Pole and the South Pole

forage: to search for and eat grass or other plants

frost line: the point underground that frost reaches down to in winter

grill: a nickname for teeth or a smile

habitat: the place where a plant or animal usually lives

krill: tiny, shrimplike animals

metabolism: the process by which a plant or an animal uses food to grow and make energy

nectar: sugary liquid made by flowers. Hummingbirds, monarch butterflies, and a number of other animals drink nectar.

omnivore: an animal that eats both animals and plants

predators: creatures that kill and eat other animals

rouses: stirs or wakes up

solo: by itself

stash: a hidden place to store food and other things

subnivium: the area under the snow's surface

sustains: feeds or nourishes

topsoil: the layer of soil nearest the surface

torpor: the physical state of a slowed-down metabolism, when breathing and heart rate slow and body temperature lowers

vertical migration: the act of moving from higher to lower during a certain season or weather pattern. Some mountain goats migrate to lower altitudes, and earthworms migrate from higher to lower in the soil.

WITH WARM THOUGHTS AND LOVE FOR CLAIRE,
EVIE, ISAAC, ROWAN, AND SADIE! —L.P.S.

TO MY SON EMMANUEL, I LOVE YOU MORE THAN
WORDS CAN EXPRESS —C.G.

Millbrook Press™
An imprint of Lerner Publishing Group, Inc.
241 First Avenue North
Minneapolis, MN 55401 USA

For reading levels and more information, look up this title at www.lernerbooks.com.

Designed by Lindsey Owens.
Main body text set in Veronika LT Std 19/23.
Typeface provided by Linotype AG.
The illustrations in this book were created with soft pastels on sanded paper with accents of silver or
copper leaf.

Library of Congress Cataloging-in-Publication Data

Names: Salas, Laura Purdie, author. | Gévry, Claudine, illustrator.
Title: Snack, snooze, skedaddle : how animals get ready for winter / Laura Purdie Salas ; illustrated by
    Claudine Gévry.
Description: Minneapolis : Millbrook Press, [2019] | Audience: Age 5–9. | Audience: K to Grade 3.
Identifiers: LCCN 2018049353 (print) | LCCN 2018050488 (ebook) | ISBN 9781541560970 (eb pdf) |
    ISBN 9781541529007 (lb : alk. paper)
Subjects: LCSH: Animals—Wintering—Juvenile literature.
Classification: LCC QL753 (ebook) | LCC QL753 .S265 2019 (print) | DDC 591.56—dc23

LC record available at https://lccn.loc.gov/2018049353

Manufactured in the United States of America
1-44767-35704-2/6/2019